Baker

Tim Wood
Photographs: Chris Fairclough

Franklin Watts
London/New York/Sydney/Toronto

I am a baker.

Every morning I pour flour down a chute into a mixer below.

I crumble yeast into tiny pieces and add it to the flour.

I add water
to the yeast and flour.
Everything goes into the mixer.

After ten minutes,
the mixer has made the dough.

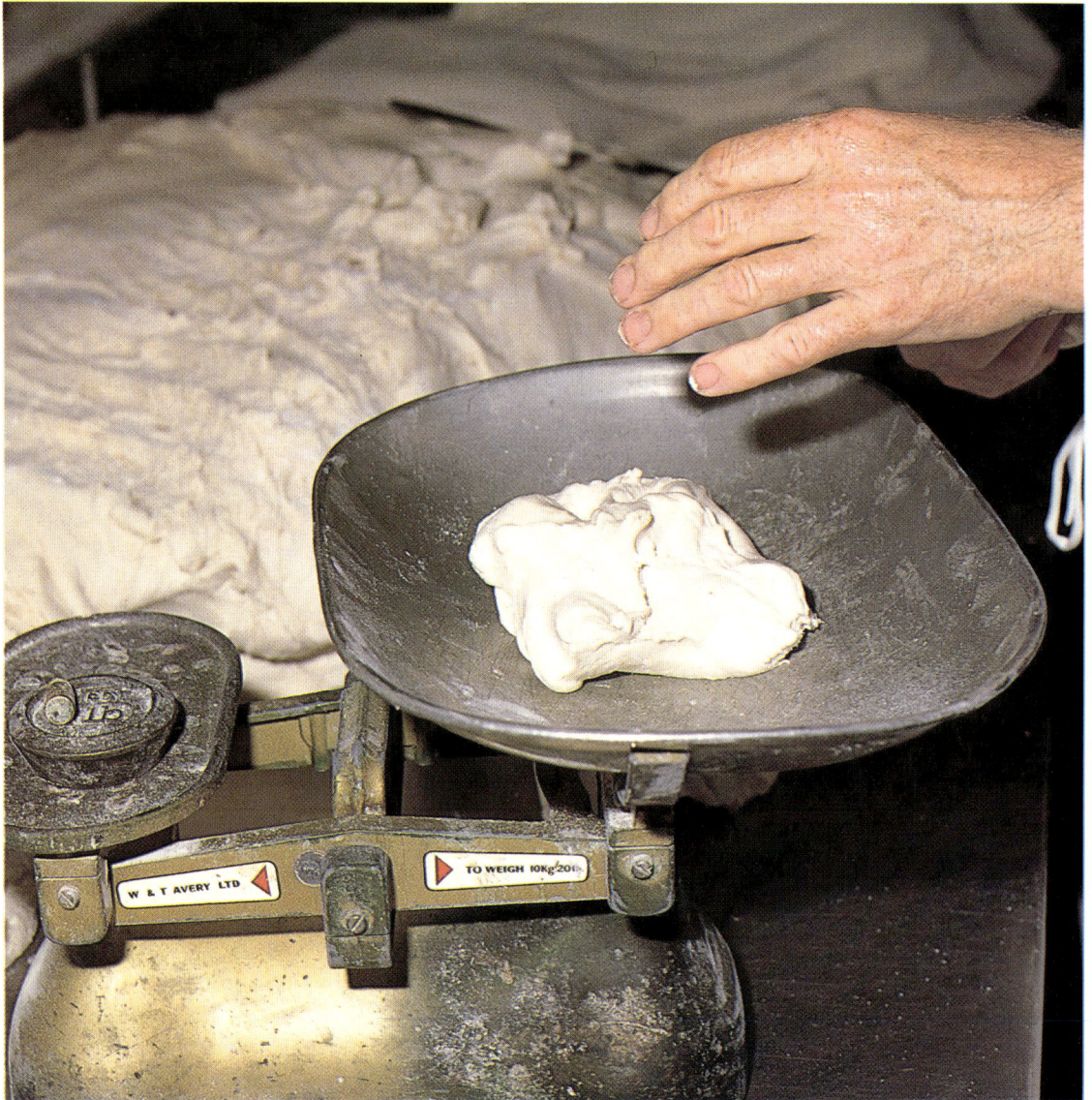

I cut up the dough
and weigh each piece carefully.

Then I knead the dough to get rid of any bubbles.

I leave the balls of dough
on trays to let them rise.

I grease the bread tins
with oil.

A machine rolls the dough into long sausage shapes.

I put each piece of dough
into a tin.

I put the tins into the hot oven using a peel.

When the bread is baked I take it out of the oven.

I tip the loaves
into a wire tray to cool.

Sometimes I make cottage loaves.

Sometimes I make plaited loaves.

Sometimes I make rolls.

Some loaves are baked
on flat trays.

Some loaves are baked in tins with lids.

The bread is ready.
My wife puts it on the shelves.
It is time to open our shop.

FACTS ABOUT BREAD AND BAKERS

Bread has been the main food of humans for at least 5,000 years.

About 10 million loaves of bread are eaten every day in Britain. Most of the wheat used to make British bread is grown in Britain.

The British spend about two thousand million pounds on bread each year.

Nearly three-quarters of the bread we eat is white bread. The rest is either brown bread or special bread such as rolls and fruit or malt loaves.

The longest loaf ever made was baked in Mexico in 1985. It was nearly 650m long and weighed over 1000 kilos.

The equipment a baker needs includes scales for weighing the yeast and dough, a thermometer for checking the temperature of the dough, a measuring jug, and brushes for cleaning up.

27

GLOSSARY

Chute
A large funnel which sends flour into a mixer.

Cottage loaf
A loaf which looks like a small round loaf on top of a large round loaf.

Dough
The mixture of flour, yeast and water from which bread is made.

Flour
Wheat which has been ground to a fine powder.

Knead
A way of rolling dough to get out all the gas bubbles.

Peel
A long wooden tool used by bakers to put baking tins into the back of a hot oven.

Plaited loaf
A loaf made by plaiting three long pieces of dough together.

Yeast
A plant which produces a gas called carbon dioxide. When yeast, flour and water are mixed together to make dough, the gas produced by the yeast makes bubbles in the dough. These bubbles make the dough rise and get bigger.

INDEX